Explore new ideas!

Welcome to the
Reading/Writing
Workshop

Read and reread exciting literature or informational texts!

Become an expert writer!

Use what you have learned to unlock the Wonders of reading!

(tl) Jupiterimages/Foodpix/Getty Images; (cb) Universal Stopping Point Photography/Flickr/Getty Images; (ct) Robin Boyer; (b) Nathan Love

Go Digital! www.connected.mcgraw-hill.com
Explore your Interactive Reading/Writing Workshop.

Mc Graw Hill **Education**

Bothell, WA • Chicago, IL • Columbus, OH • New York, NY

Cover and Title Pages: Nathan Love

www.mheonline.com/readingwonders

C

Education

Copyright © 2014 The McGraw-Hill Companies, Inc.

All rights reserved. No part of this publication may be reproduced or distributed in any form or by any means, or stored in a database or retrieval system, without the prior written consent of The McGraw-Hill Companies, Inc., including, but not limited to, network storage or transmission, or broadcast for distance learning.

Send all inquiries to:
McGraw-Hill Education
Two Penn Plaza
New York, New York 10121

ISBN: 978-0-02-119728-6
MHID: 0-02-119728-8

Printed in the United States of America.

4 5 6 7 8 9 RJE 17 16 15 14 13

McGraw-Hill Reading Wonders

CCSS Reading/Language Arts Program

Program Authors

Diane August

Donald R. Bear

Janice A. Dole

Jana Echevarria

Douglas Fisher

David Francis

Vicki Gibson

Jan Hasbrouck

Margaret Kilgo

Jay McTighe

Scott G. Paris

Timothy Shanahan

Josefina V. Tinajero

McGraw Hill Education

Bothell, WA • Chicago, IL • Columbus, OH • New York, NY

Unit 2

Our Community

The Big Idea

What makes a community?. **6**

Week 1 · Jobs Around Town   8

Words to Know 10
Phonics: Short e 12
Good Job, Ben!
    Realistic Fiction .14
Comprehension Skill: Character, Setting, Events. . 24
Writing and Grammar: Organization/Nouns 26

Week 2 · Buildings All Around   28

Words to Know 30
Phonics: Short u 32
Cubs in a Hut
    Fantasy 34
Comprehension Skill: Character, Setting,
Events 44
Writing and Grammar: Organization/
Plural Nouns 46

(t) Diane Greenseid; (c) Robin Boyer; (b) Amanda Gulliver

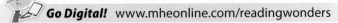

Go Digital! www.mheonline.com/readingwonders

Week 3 · A Community in Nature 48

Words to Know 50
Phonics: End Blends 52
The Best Spot
Nonfiction 54
Comprehension Skill: Main Topic and
Key Details. 64
Writing and Grammar: Ideas/Possessive
Nouns. 66

Week 4 · Let's Help 68

Words to Know 70
Phonics: th, sh, -ng 72
Thump Thump Helps Out
Fantasy 74
Comprehension Skill: Character, Setting, Events. . 84
Writing and Grammar: Organization/
Proper Nouns. 86

Week 5 · Follow the Map 88

Words to Know 90
Phonics: ch, -tch, wh, ph 92
Which Way on the Map?
Nonfiction 94
Comprehension Skill: Main Topic and Key Details . . . 104
Writing and Grammar: Ideas/Irregular
Plural Nouns 106

(t) Universal Stopping Point Photography/Flickr/Getty Images; (b) Sergio de Giorgio

Unit 2
Our Community

Diane Greenseid

On My Street

Houses standing in a row,
One of them is mine, I know.

Many families on one street,
Each with friends it's
fun to meet.

Everywhere I look I see,
This neighborhood is
home to me.

—Constance Andrea Keremes

The Big Idea

What makes a community?

Essential Question

What jobs need to be done in a community?

Go Digital!

At Work

Talk About It

How is this man's work important in the community?

Fuse/Getty Images

again

I may need to bake it **again.**

help

She will **help** find the street.

new

My class has a **new** teacher.

Read Together

there

There is a lot of mail in his bag.

use

Use a scoop to pick up the rocks.

Your Turn

COLLABORATE

Say the sentence for each word. Then make up another sentence.

Go Digital! *Use the online visual glossary*

(tl) Bananastock/Alamy; (cl) Masterfile; (bl) Corbis; (tr) Design Pics Inc./Alamy; (br) Steve Allen/Brand X Pictures/Getty Images

Short e

The letters e or ea can make the short e sound, as in **get** or **bread**.

men	**vet**	**pet**
bed	**red**	**mess**
head	**well**	**dress**
smell	**deaf**	**bread**

Robin Boyer

Fred's pet hen can peck!

The top of its head is red.

Your Turn

Look for these words with the short e sound in "Good Job, Ben!"

Ben	head	get	yet
men	wet	step	bread
smells	ten	Jet	vet
well	pet	Glenn	read

Essential Question

What jobs need to be done in a community?

Read about jobs that people do around town.

Go Digital!

Robin Boyer

14

Good Job, Ben!

Ben and Mom head to town.
It is a big trip.
There is a lot to see.

Robin Boyer

Ben and Mom will get on the bus.
The driver stops on this block.

Good job!

Ben and Mom can not cross yet.
Stop! Stop! She can **help** them.

Big job!

Robin Boyer

Ben and Mom walk past.
Six men **use** a drill and fill cracks.
It will look **new again**.

Wet job!

Ben and Mom step in for bread.
Ben sniffs. It smells good.
Mom gets ten.

Hot job!

Robin Boyer

Ben and Mom get Jet.

Jet licks Ben.

The vet helped Jet get well quick.

Pet job!

Ben and Mom stop for books.
Ben can get help from Miss Glenn.

Glad job!

Robin Boyer

What did Ben get?
What has he read?
Ben read books on jobs.

Good job, Ben!

Character, Setting, Events

A **character** is a person or animal in a story.

The **setting** is where a story takes place.

The **events** are what happen in a story.

🔍 Find Text Evidence

Find the characters, the setting, and an event.

page 16

(Ben and Mom) (head to town.)
It is a big trip.
There is a lot to see.

Robin Boyer

24

Characters	Setting	Events
Ben Mom	at the bus stop	They are going to town.
Ben Mom	bakery	They buy bread.
Ben Mom	library	Ben finds books about jobs.

Your Turn

COLLABORATE

Talk about other characters, settings, and events in "Good Job, Ben!"

Go Digital! *Use the interactive graphic organizer*

Readers to...

Organization Jeff came up with a good idea for a story. Then he thought about how to tell it.

Jeff's Story

Ned sells caps and bats.

Tess gets a new red cap.

COLLABORATE

Your Turn

Tell how Jeff organized his story.

Writers

Nouns A noun names a person, place, or thing. The word **cap** is a noun.

Tess gets a new red **cap**.

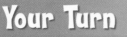

Your Turn

COLLABORATE

- Find another noun in Jeff's story.
- Write new sentences. Circle the noun in each sentence.

Robin Boyer

Essential Question

What buildings do you know?
What are they made of?

Go Digital!

Sakis Papadopoulos/Robert Harding World Imagery/Getty Images

Our Town

Talk About It

What kinds of buildings are in this city?

could

They **could** build a house with logs.

live

Do you **live** in a tall building?

one

This hut has **one** room.

then

We open the door, and **then** we go out.

three

Three people can fit in a tent.

(tl) Image Source/Getty Images; (cl) Ben Bloom/Photodisc/Getty Images; (bl) MIXA/Getty Images; (tr) Kiyotaka Kitajima/amanaimages/Corbis; (br) imagebroker/Alamy

Your Turn

COLLABORATE

Say the sentence for each word. Then make up another sentence.

Go Digital! *Use the online visual glossary*

Short <u>u</u>

The letter u can make the
short u sound in **hut**.

<u>u</u>p	f<u>u</u>n	b<u>u</u>t
b<u>u</u>s	c<u>u</u>p	d<u>u</u>ck
b<u>u</u>g	dr<u>u</u>m	m<u>u</u>d
t<u>u</u>b	t<u>u</u>cked	st<u>u</u>ff

Amanda Gulliver

Buzz the bug can live in mud.

But can Buzz run and have fun?

Your Turn

COLLABORATE

Look for these words with short u in
"Cubs in a Hut."

cubs	hut	Gus	mud
Russ	fun	Bud	up
rugs	stuff	us	snug
bugs	rug		

Essential Question

**What buildings do you know?
What are they made of?**

Read about how three cubs
build a hut.

Go Digital!

Amanda Gulliver

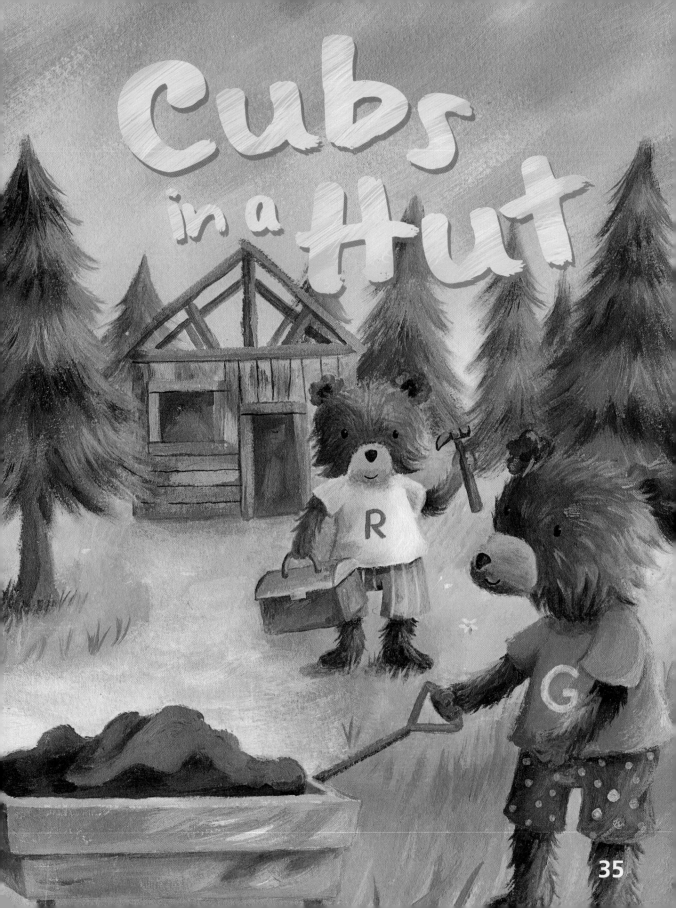

Cubs in a Hut

Amanda Gulliver

"Let's make a hut," said Gus.

"We **could** use mud," said Russ.

"It will be fun!" said Bud.

The cubs had a plan.
Bud got a big stack of sticks.
Russ and Gus got mud
and grass.

The cubs did a very good job.

"Let's move in!" yelled Russ.

"Yes, yes!" yelled Bud and Gus.

Amanda Gulliver

The cubs set up rugs and beds.
They filled up the hut with lots
of stuff.

Then **one** night **three** cubs got up.

Drip, drip, drip!

"My bed is wet!" yelled Bud.

Amanda Gulliver

"My head is wet!" yelled Gus.

"It's not fun to **live** in a wet hut!" yelled Russ.

"We must fix it," said Bud.

"It will not drip on us," said Gus.

"We will not get wet," said Russ.

Amanda Gulliver

It is good to live in a dry hut.
Three cubs are as snug as bugs
in a rug!

Character, Setting, Events

A **character** is a person or animal in a story.

The **setting** is where a story takes place.

The **events** are what happen in a story.

Find Text Evidence

Use the words and the pictures to find a character, setting, and event in the story.

page 37

The cubs had a plan.
Bud got a big stack of sticks.
Russ and Gus got mud
and grass.

Amanda Gulliver

Character	Setting	Events
Bud	forest	He got sticks.
Russ	forest	He got mud.
Gus	forest	He got grass.

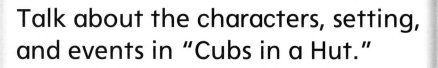

COLLABORATE

Your Turn

Talk about the characters, setting, and events in "Cubs in a Hut."

Go Digital! *Use the interactive graphic organizer*

Organization Judd wrote a story with a beginning, middle, and end.

Judd's Story

Six ducks lived in mud huts.

The mud huts fell down.

They used bricks to fix them.

Now the ducks have good huts!

Your Turn

COLLABORATE

Tell what happens in the beginning, middle, and end of Judd's story.

Amanda Gulliver

Writers

Plural Nouns A **plural** means more than one. Most plural words end in -**s**. The noun **ducks** is plural.

Six **ducks** lived in mud huts.

COLLABORATE

Your Turn

- Find more plurals in Judd's story.
- Write new sentences with plural words.

Essential Question

Where do animals live together?

Go Digital!

Peter Scoones/Taxi/Getty Images

Animals at Home

Talk About It

What kind of place do these animals live in?

eat

Chipmunks like to **eat** nuts.

no

A snake has **no** legs.

of

The birds sit in a nest **of** twigs.

under

They dive down **under** the water.

who

Who can see the bug?

(tl) David R. Frazier Photolibrary/Alamy; (cl) IT Stock/PunchStock; (bl) Gary Neil Corbett/ SuperStock; (tr) Stephan Zabel/Getty Images; (br) Jamie Grill/Corbis

Your Turn

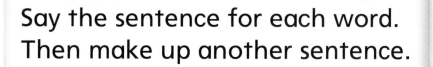

Say the sentence for each word.
Then make up another sentence.

Go Digital! *Use the online visual glossary*

End Blends

The letters nd, nk, nt, sk, st, and mp together make the ending sounds in **land**, **drink**, **went**, **ask**, **rest**, and **damp**.

and	**fast**	**jump**
send	**desk**	**must**
hunt	**mask**	**plant**
skunk	**trunk**	**stamp**

Margie Moore

The sk<u>u</u><u>n</u>k is pl<u>u</u><u>mp</u> a<u>nd</u> fa<u>st</u>!

It will play a<u>nd</u> hu<u>nt</u>.

Your Turn

COLLABORATE

Look for these words with end blends in "The Best Spot."

be<u>st</u>	pla<u>nt</u>s	ne<u>st</u>
tru<u>nk</u>	a<u>nt</u>s	a<u>nd</u>
re<u>st</u>	sa<u>nd</u>	stu<u>mp</u>
ju<u>mp</u>	mu<u>st</u>	hu<u>nt</u>s
du<u>sk</u>	we<u>nt</u>	sku<u>nk</u>

Essential Question

Where do animals live together?

Read about the animals in a forest.

Go Digital!

The Best Spot

(t-b) by Tom Vezo/Minden Pictures; Gail Shumway/Photographer's Choice/Getty Images

Shin Yoshino/Minden Pictures; (border) Carl Keyes/Alamy

This is a forest.

This spot has lots **of** animals.

Deer live here. They **eat** plants.

But **who** is in the grass?

A rabbit's head pops up!

Universal Stopping Point Photography/Flickr/Getty Images

(bkgd) Pixtal/age fotostock; (inset) Dave Cole/Alamy; (border) Carl Keyes/Alamy

What is up there?

Look up, up, up.

It is a nest.

The mom gets big bugs. Yum!

What is on the trunk?

It is a nest, too.

Lots of wasps live in it.

(t to b) Philippe Clement/Nature Picture Library; IT Stock Free/Alamy

Ants live here, too.

Ants pick up twigs and grass.

Ants zip in and out.

Ants have **no** rest!

Zoonar GmbH/Alamy; (border) Carl Keyes/Alamy

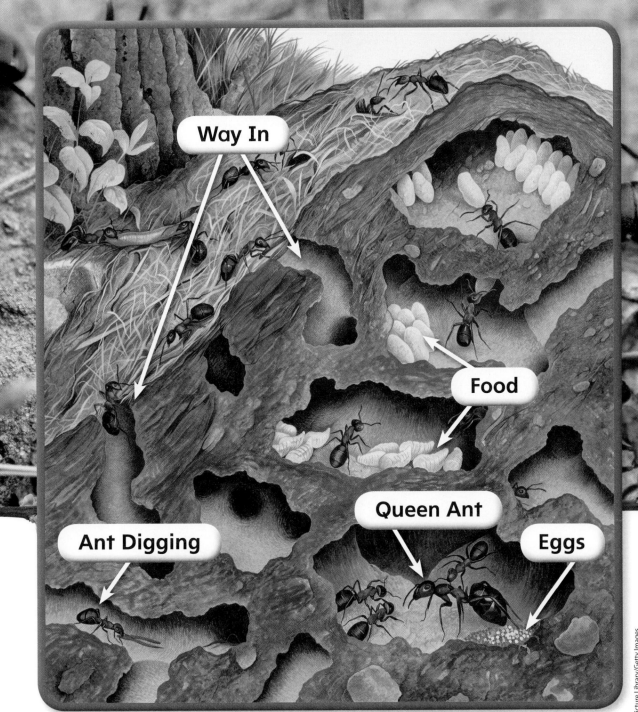

Ants dig **under** sand and grass.

DEA Picture Library/De Agostini Picture Library/Getty Images

Fox kits hop on a stump.

Mom fox lets the kits run and jump.

The kits must eat.

Dad fox hunts at dusk.

tbkmedia.de/Alamy; (border) Carl Keyes/Alamy

Who went hunting, too?
A skunk!

This spot has lots of animals!

Comstock/PunchStock

Main Topic and Key Details

The **main topic** is what the selection is about.

Key details give information about the main topic.

Find Text Evidence

The selection is about a place where animals live together.

Find a detail about one of the animals.

page 56

This is a forest.

This spot has lots **of** animals.

Deer live here. They **eat** plants.

Shin Yoshino/Minden Pictures

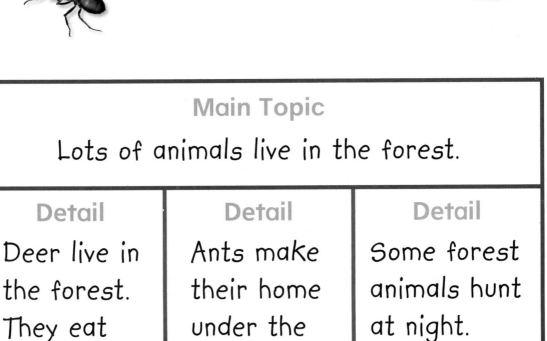

Main Topic

Lots of animals live in the forest.

Detail	Detail	Detail
Deer live in the forest. They eat plants.	Ants make their home under the ground.	Some forest animals hunt at night.

Your Turn

COLLABORATE

Talk about the main topic and other details in "The Best Spot."

Go Digital! *Use the interactive graphic organizer*

Zoonar GmbH/Alamy

Readers to...

Ideas Brent decided on an idea.
Then he wrote sentences to explain it.

Brent's Sentences

Lots of animals live in the forest.

A cub's den is snug.

A bug's log is damp.

Your Turn

COLLABORATE

Tell what details Brent used to explain his idea.

Writers

Possessive Nouns A possessive noun tells who or what has something. A possessive noun that tells about one thing ends with **'s**.

A **cub's** den is snug.

Your Turn

COLLABORATE

- Find another possessive noun in Brent's sentences.
- Write new sentences with possessive nouns.

Margie Moore

Make It Better

Talk About It

What are these children doing together to make a difference?

all

Let's pick up **all** the trash.

call

Who will you **call** to help?

day

It is a good **day** to plant.

her

Mom recycles **her** bottles.

want

I **want** to help my Gram.

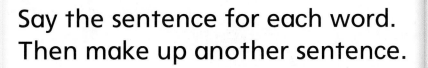

Your Turn

COLLABORATE

Say the sentence for each word. Then make up another sentence.

Go Digital! Use the online visual glossary

(tl) Leland Bobb£/Corbis; (c) STOCK4B GmbH/Alamy; (bl) Maria Spann/Photographer's Choice/Getty Images; (tr) Image Source/Alamy (br) Jose Luis Pelaez/Getty Images

th, sh, -ng

The letters th make the sound you hear in **that** or **path**.

The letters sh make the sound you hear in **shop** or **fish**.

The letters -ng make the sound you hear in **ring**.

then	**shut**	**wing**
math	**thank**	**hang**
shed	**sing**	**crash**
with	**fresh**	**sting**

Sergio DeGiorgi

I bang my drum on this ship.

Can Beth sing a song?

Your Turn

COLLABORATE

Look for these words with th, sh, and -ng in "Thump Thump Helps Out."

thump	thumped	sang
hush	that	bang
crash	wish	Sheldon
think	rushed	long
with	song	brings this

Essential Question

How do people help out in the community?

Go Digital!

Sergio DeGiorgi

Thump Thump Helps Out

Thump Thump liked to thump.

He thumped a lot as he sang.

He thumped a lot just for fun.

Sergio DeGiorgi

"Hush! Stop that, Thump Thump!" yelled **all** the little rabbits.

"We do not like it one bit!"

But Thump Thump did not stop.

One **day**, there was a problem.

Thump Thump's bus hit a rock.

Bang! Crash! Clunk!

His bus got stuck in the mud.

The little rabbits could not fix it.

Sergio DeGiorgi

"We wish big rabbits could get us home," sniffed the little rabbits.

"Help us!" yelled Miss Sheldon.

But not one big rabbit heard **her call**.

Thump Thump had a plan.

"I think I can help," he sang.

He thumped and thumped and thumped.

Sergio DeGiorgi

Big rabbits all over heard
Thump Thump's thump.

They rushed to help fix the bus.

The kids got home fast.

"Thump Thump, can you help us?" asked the big rabbits.

"We **want** you to thump loud and long if a rabbit needs help."

Sergio DeGiorgi

"Thump, Thump!" went Thump
Thump, with a song.

And Thump Thump thumps and
brings help to this day.

Character, Setting, Events

A **character** is a person or animal in a story.

The **setting** is where a story takes place.

The **events** are what happen in a story.

Find Text Evidence

Use the words and pictures to find the events that happen in the story.

page 76

Thump Thump liked to thump.

He thumped a lot as he sang.

He thumped a lot just for fun.

Sergio DeGiorgi

Characters	Setting	Events
Thump Thump	forest	He thumped his feet a lot.
Rabbits	forest	The bus hit a rock and got stuck in the mud.
Thump Thump	forest	He thumped his feet to get help.

Your Turn

COLLABORATE

Talk about the characters, setting, and events in "Thump Thump Helps Out."

Go Digital! *Use the interactive graphic organizer*

Readers to...

Organization Trish wrote a story with a beginning, a middle, and an end.

Trish's Story

King Beach is a big mess!

Seth and Liz pick up trash.

Now the beach

is clean!

Your Turn

Tell what happens in the beginning, middle, and end of Trish's story.

Writers

Proper Nouns A **proper noun** begins with a capital letter. The name of the place **King Beach** is a proper noun.

King Beach is a big mess!

Your Turn
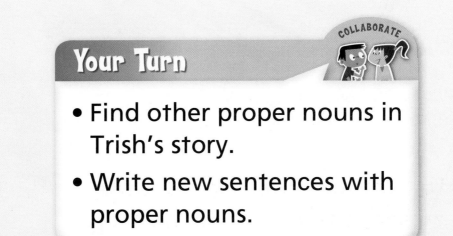

- Find other proper nouns in Trish's story.

- Write new sentences with proper nouns.

87

Sergio DeGiorgi

Essential Question

How can you find your way around?

Go Digital!

Jeff Greenberg/Alamy

Map It!

COLLABORATE

Talk About It

What is the family using to get directions?

around

I like to ride **around** the park.

by

The bus stops **by** my house.

many

There are **many** shops in town.

place

Let's look for this **place** on a map.

walk

We **walk** to the library.

(tl) Petr Bonek/Alamy; (cl) Tom Rosenthal/SuperStock; (bl) Holger Leue/ Lonely Planet Images/Getty Images; (tr) Jack Hollingsworth/Digital Vision/ Getty Images; (br) opus/a.collectionRF/Getty Images

Your Turn

COLLABORATE

Say the sentence for each word. Then make up another sentence.

Go Digital! **Use the online visual glossary**

<u>ch</u>, -<u>tch</u>, <u>wh</u>, <u>ph</u>

The letters <u>ch</u> and -<u>tch</u> make the sound you hear in **chop** and **catch**.

The letters <u>wh</u> make the sound you hear in **when**.

The letters <u>ph</u> make the sound you hear in **Phil**.

in<u>ch</u>	<u>wh</u>iz	<u>ch</u>at
itch	<u>wh</u>en	gra<u>ph</u>
lun<u>ch</u>	<u>ch</u>eck	stitch
<u>wh</u>i<u>ch</u>	ske<u>tch</u>	mu<u>ch</u>

Scott Burroughs

Phil will ske<u>tch</u> a gra<u>ph</u> for math.

<u>Wh</u>en will he get his lun<u>ch</u>?

COLLABORATE

Your Turn

Look for these words with <u>ch</u>, -<u>tch</u>, <u>wh</u>, and <u>ph</u> in "Which Way on the Map?"

<u>wh</u>i<u>ch</u>   **Mi<u>tch</u>**   **Step<u>h</u>**

<u>ch</u>ildren   **<u>ch</u>at**   **ben<u>ch</u>es**

ca<u>tch</u>   **su<u>ch</u>**   **lun<u>ch</u>**   **<u>ch</u>eck**

Essential Question

How can you find your way around?

Read about places in a town.

Go Digital!

Lane Oatey/Getty Images

Which Way on the Map?

(l) Lane Oatey/Getty Images; (r) The McGraw-Hill Companies, Inc.

DAJ/Getty Images

Mitch and Steph live in a big town.

There is a lot to see.

Let's **walk around** with them.

This is the town on a map.

It shows each **place** in town.

The McGraw-Hill Companies, Inc.

This place has red bricks.

Many children go here.

Mitch and Steph go here, too.

Which place is this?

Swerve/Alamy

Can you spot it on the map?

The McGraw-Hill Companies, Inc.

This place is **by** a lake. People chat on benches. Mitch and Steph will run and play catch. It is such fun!
Which place is this?

Andrea Rugg/Beateworks/Corbis

Can you spot it on the map?

The McGraw-Hill Companies, Inc.

This place has a big box. Mitch and Steph stop and get stamps. They drop a letter in the big box. Which place is this?

Bruce Clark/Photolibrary/Getty Images

Can you spot it on the map?

Where can Mitch and Steph get lunch?

Check the map!

The McGraw-Hill Companies, Inc.

Main Topic and Key Details

The **main topic** is what the selection is about.

Key details give information about the main topic.

Find Text Evidence

The selection is about how to use a map.

Find a detail about the school in Mitch and Steph's town.

page 98

This place has red bricks.

Swerve/Alamy

Main Topic		
How to Use a Map to Find Places in Town		
Detail	**Detail**	**Detail**
The school has red bricks. The school is on the map.	The playground is by the lake. The playground is on the map.	The post office has a big box. The post office is on the map.

Your Turn

COLLABORATE

Talk about the main topic and details in "Which Way on the Map?"

Go Digital! **Use the interactive graphic organizer**

The McGraw-Hill Companies, Inc.

Readers to...

Ideas Chad decided on an idea. Then he wrote sentences to explain details about it.

Chad's Sentences

This hat shop is by a bank.

It sells ball caps for children.

It sells sports hats for

men and women, too.

COLLABORATE

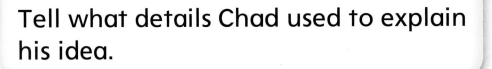

Your Turn

Tell what details Chad used to explain his idea.

Writers

Irregular Plural Nouns Some nouns that name more than one do not end in **-s** or **-es**.

It sells ball caps for **children**.

Your Turn

COLLABORATE

- Look at Chad's sentences. Find another plural noun that does not end in **-s** or **-es**.

- Write a new sentence using a plural noun that does not end in **-s** or **-es**.

Scott Burroughs